# THIS IS A
# MOOSE

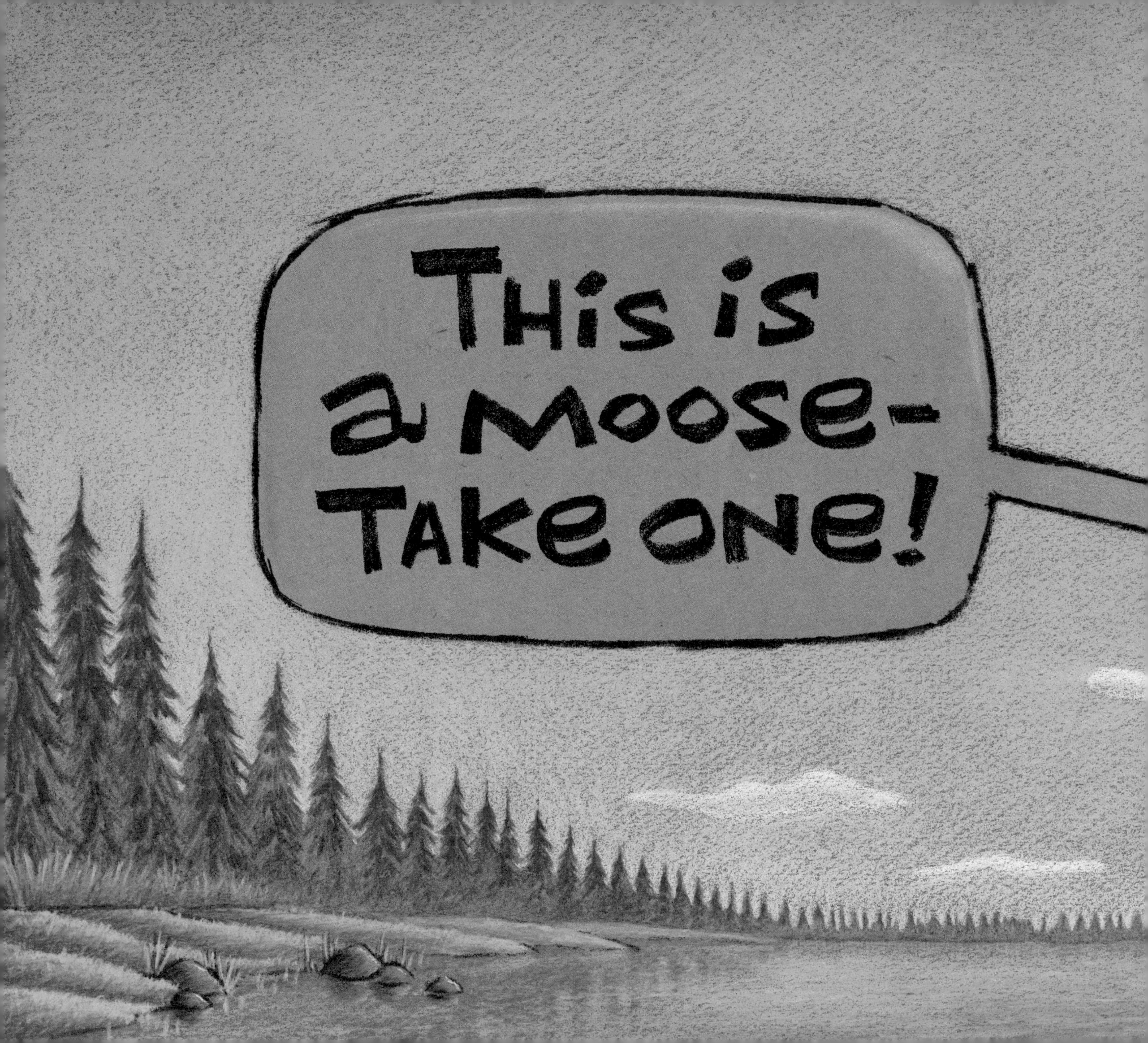
This is a moose-Take one!

# THIS IS A MOOSE

RICHARD T. MORRIS IS AN AUTHOR.

TOM LICHTENHELD IS AN ILLUSTRATOR.

SCHOLASTIC INC.

This
is the
Mighty
Moose.

His father
is a moose.

His mother
is a moose.

This moose wants to be an astronaut.

Excuse me, but moose cannot be astronauts.
Moose are large, hoofed animals that live in the woods. Now, would someone kindly get the moose out of the space suit? Thank you.

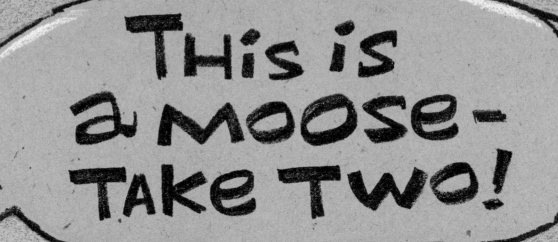

# This is the Mighty Moose.

His father is a moose.

His mother is a...

Enter the grandmother.

THIS IS A MOOSE - TAKE THREE!
THIS IS A MOOSE
DIR.: BILLY WADDLER
3
SCENE: MOOSE INTRO
CAM.: CHIP N. ZEE
OW!

This is the Mighty Moose.

His father
is a moose.

His mother...

Behold, the Regal Giraffe.
Actually, I've always wanted to be a doctor....

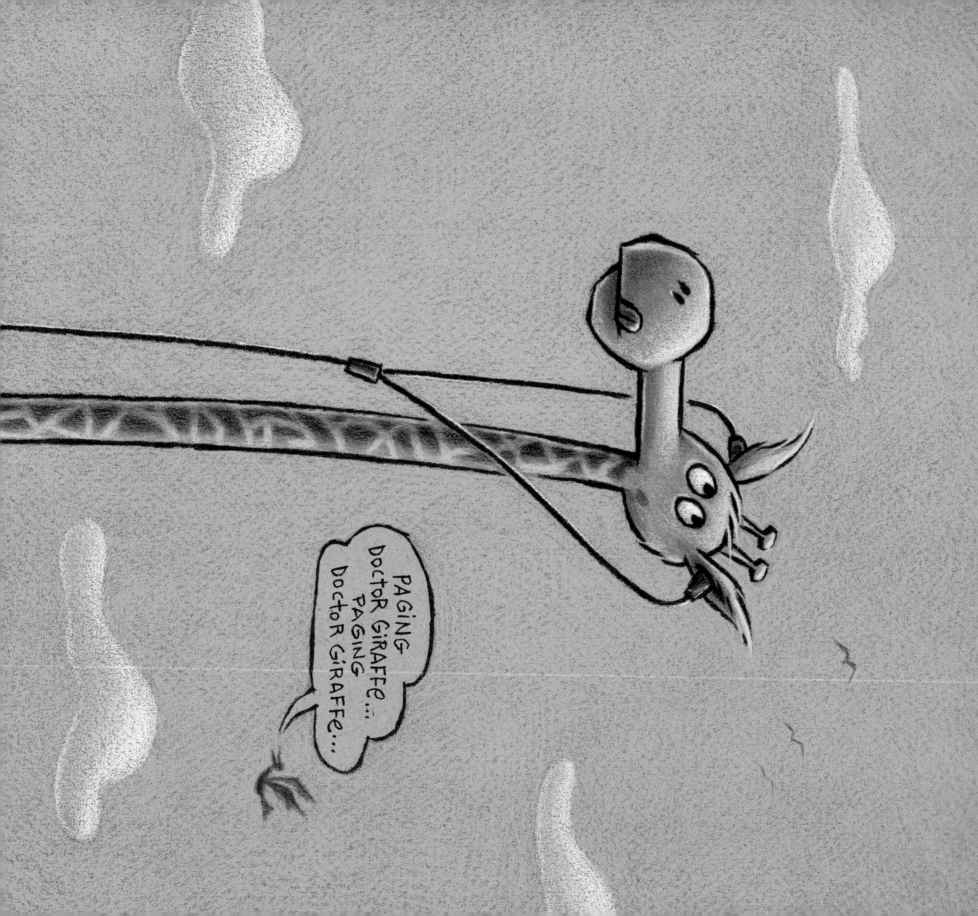

Grandmother Moose
and Regal Giraffe

prepare to launch
Mighty Moose into space.

GO, MOOSE!

MOON OR BUST!

Look at that moose go!

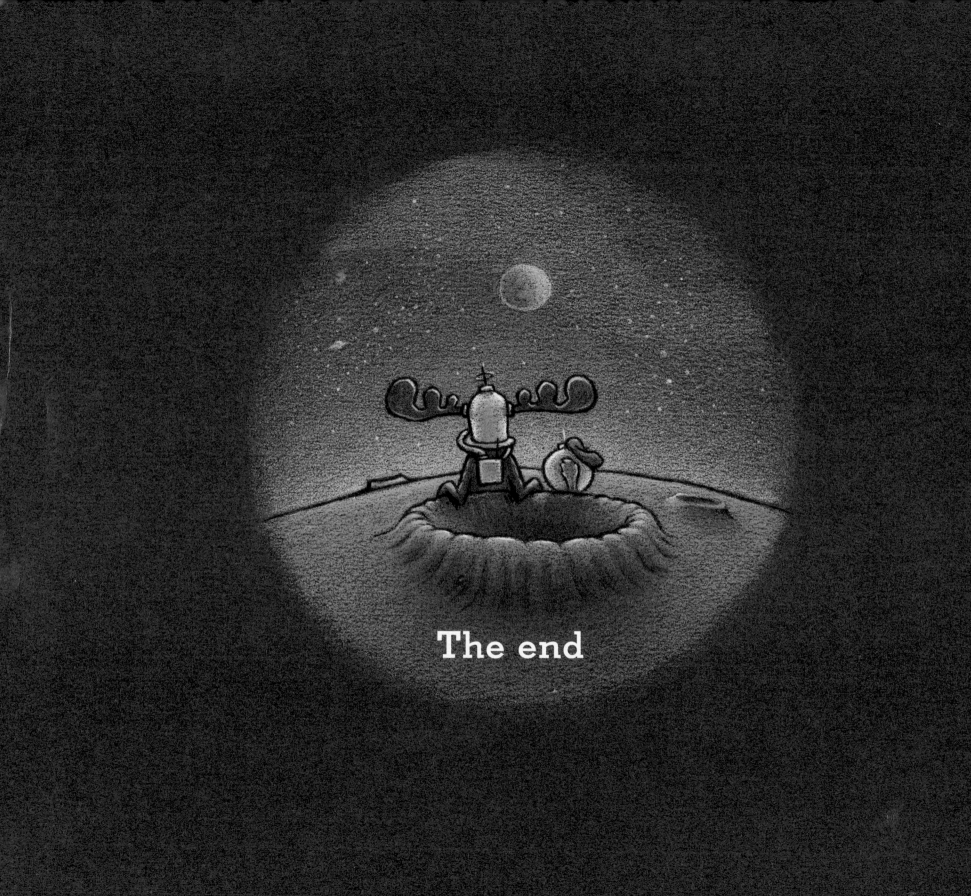

The end